A STUDY AND CONCEPT

OF

ENTREPRENEURSHIP

:: Author ::

Dr. Chirag V. Raval

(M.COM., M.phil, Ph.D)

PUBLISHED BY

The New ERa International Publishing House
H.Q. At & Po. Chaveli., Ta- Chansma,
Dist- Patan, North Gujarat, India, Asia.
www.iphouseindia.com

First Publication: 6th December, 2014

Copyright: Author

(c) **Dr. Chirag Raval**

ISBN:- 978-15-08473-00-8

Price: Rs.750/- INDIA

$ 15 OUTSIDE INDIA

PUBLISHED BY

The New ERa International Publishing House
H.Q. At & Po. Chaveli., Ta- Chansma,
Dist- Patan, North Gujarat, India, Asia.
www.iphouseindia.com

Contents

1. INTRODUCTION

The liberalization of Indian economy in the 1990s has paved the way for a huge number of people to become entrepreneurs.

Globalisation has positively affected Indian entrepreneurship. Indians have beaten foreign companies. A large number of Indian entrepreneurs are emerging in the global market. India is second amongst all nations in total entrepreneurship activity as per the "Global Entrepreneurship Monitor Report".

The global economy is a borderless world economy, characterised by free flow of trade and factors of production across national borders. The world economy has been emerging as a global economy. A global economy is one which transcends the national borders unhindered by artificial restrictions like government restrictions on trade and factor movement. Globalisation is a process of development of the world into a single integrated economic unit.

EVOLUTION OF THE TERM ENTREPRENEUR:

By its root the word 'entrepreneur' dates back to 16th century. At that time, in the European countries it was used in a sense close to the modern concept of 'adventurer'. The leaders of risky military expeditions and also the daredevils, capable of organising and heading enterprises calculated on chance success, were called as entrepreneurs.

Hundred years later, the interpretation of the term does no longer coincide with the meaning given to it earlier. In narrower sense the architects, engineers, irrigators, i.e., the people from specific professions were considered as entrepreneurs and in broader sense it referred to all contractors and sub-contractors receiving credits for models, of roads, buildings, bridges, irrigational works etc. In other words, the concept of 'entrepreneur' was gradually applied to the agents in financial practice efficiently utilising the loan resources. As if taking cognizance of the useful significance of entrepreneurial activities, the European public opinion of new era attached a different adjective to the notion of money in general and 'idle wealth' in particular - capitalist.

This rigid definition of the term used for designating various subdivisions of the predominant class was retained till the end of 18th century. Later on, as capitalism turned into an all-pervading system of economy, in which a mechanism of productive utilisation of accumulations took shape, there occurred a combination of and imposition on each other of the various earlier concepts. One reservation is required at this point though; French political economics gave a new life to the word 'entrepreneur'.

In the second half of 18th century a scholar-cum-banker R. Cantillion expanded it to 'trade professions', by including the 'middlemen making profits out of the difference margin of prices on wholesale and retail goods in the rank of entrepreneurs.

The representatives of classical school of bourgeois political economy (Physiocrats' school) considered it possible to include as part of them the big landowners productively utilising their wealth. The forefather of another of its school- the school of vulgar political economy- J. B. Say supplemented his idea about entrepreneur as an active subject of market economy with the traits, which in totality transformed into its invariable characteristics. In more complete form they were formulated in his "Catechism of political economy," originally published in France, but soon translated into other European languages.

The author of "Catechism" referred all the agents of market economy who received profit on invested capital by productive means to the category of entrepreneurs. He thought that an entrepreneur was bound to create job placements, produce goods and services. His function was to combine the factors of production into one whole and to be able to direct them.

Thus, in spite of divergence in definitions, the French economics worked out a common conceptual approach to the content of the concept 'entrepreneur'. It gradually expanded this term to all active market agents receiving profit by productive means in contrast to money by the traders. As a result, the adjective derived from the word 'capital' started to be used for the term 'entrepreneur' became a synonym of the expression "active capitalist". It was used in this sense by Karl Marx, who created an image of a 'capitalist entrepreneur' that personified typical characteristics of industrial production at the stage of pre-monopolist and the first decade of monopolist capitalism. The "active" businessman was compelled to act by his own distinctive image, but in the opinion of the founder of the theory of Marxism, the fundamental tendencies of development of capitalist production is competition and accumulation.

DEFINITIONS OF ENTREPRENEUR:

The concept of entrepreneur has been defined through different definitions.

- Person who undertake commercial venture - Oxford Dictionary.

- Minimum input, maximum output and quality maintains that person entrepreneur.

5

- Entrepreneur is a change agent. He searches and accepts innovation.

- The person who establishes and manages a business and bears risk or uncertainty and earns profit (or loss) for it is called an entrepreneur. It is he who arranges all factors of production and makes decisions regarding production and makes payments of rewards to factors of production for their services. - Dictionary of Management.

- The new encyclopaedia Britanica"- Considers an entrepreneur as an individual who bears the risk of operating a business in the face of uncertainty about the future conditions."

- **Franci A. Walker's Views on Entrepreneur:** According to walker, the true entrepreneur is one who is endowed with more than average capacities in the task of organising and co-coordinating the factors of production, like land, labour and capital, besides his own inputs as an entrepreneur. He is looked upon as the captain of an industry, a pioneer, who, through his vision, brings about a rapid growth of his organisation.

The surplus reward that he receives is ascribable to his superior talent.

- **Rechard Cantillon's Theory of 'Risk-Bearing':** The classical economists led by Adam Smith did not have a clear idea about entrepreneurship. Words like adventurer, undertaker and projector were used in the writings of Adam Smith, Pigou and other classical economists. It was "Richard Cantillon (1680-1734)", the Irish economist who first used the term entrepreneur to refer to economic activities."

Richard Cantillon viewed entrepreneurs as risk-bearing agents of production. According to him "an entrepreneur is one who buys factors of production at certain prices, combines the factors of production into a product and sells the product at an uncertain price.

- **J. B. Say's Theory of Co-ordination, Organisation and Supervision:** J. B. Say makes a distinction between the capitalist and the entrepreneur. He considers the capitalist as the financier and the entrepreneur as an organizer.

According to J. B. Say, "an entrepreneur is one who coordinates and organizes the resources and oversees the activities of the enterprise to produce the required goods/services. The entrepreneur combines the land owned by one person, the capital offered by another person and the labour of yet another person and produces a product.

- **Schumpeter's Theory of 'Innovation':** Schumpeter visualised entrepreneur as an innovator. He considers a person an entrepreneur, if the person acts as a catalyst by his innovative ideas and actions and introduces dynamism in the economy, thereby interrupting and altering the stagnant circular flow of the economy and bringing about development. He considers that innovation can take the following forms:

- Introduction of a new product.
- Introduction of a new, improved technology for the production of an existing product.

- Opening of a new market into which a specific product has not entered so far.

- Discovery of new source of supply of raw material.

- Carrying out a new form of organization.

Going by the types of innovations enumerated by Schumpeter, a person who sets up an enterprise for producing a product that already exists in the market, making use of the existing technology and offering his product to the existing market is kept outside the definition of entrepreneur. Schumpeter argues that inventions or discoveries by themselves have little economic effect. Schumpeter also makes a distinction between an inventor and an innovator. While the inventor finds out new methods, techniques, materials, products etc., the innovator makes use of such inventions and discoveries to produce and offer new products/services to the economy. He calls the innovator as the entrepreneur.

- **Peter F. Drucker's Views on Entrepreneurs: (Theory of opportunity)**

Peter Drucker sums up the salient characteristics of an entrepreneur. He has aptly observed."Innovation is the specific tools of entrepreneurs, the means by which they exploit changes as an opportunity for a different business or different service. It is capable of being learned and practiced."

"Entrepreneurs need to search purposefully for the sources on innovation, the changes and their symptoms that indicate opportunities for successful innovation. And they need to know and to apply the principles of successful innovation."

- **New Concept of Entrepreneur:** The term entrepreneur has been defined as one who detects and evaluates a new situation in his environment and directs the making of such adjustments in the economic systems as he deems necessary. He conceives of an industrial enterprise for the purpose, displays considerable initiative, grit and determination bringing his project to fruition and in this process, performs one or more of the following.

Supplies technical knowhow, Perceives opportunities for profitable investments, Obtains necessary industrial licences, Provides personal guarantees to the financial institutions, Explores the prospects of starting such a manufacturing enterprise, Arranges initial capital and Promises to meet the shortfalls in the capital.

Who is an Entrepreneur?

E	Enterprising - calculated risk.
N	New Ideas.
T	Thorough
R	Resourceful
E	Enthusiastic
P	Problem solving attitude
R	Rapport establishment with customers, bankers, suppliers.
E	Effective
N	Novel attitude to achieve higher aims
E	Engine for motivating personnel
U	Understanding
R	Receptive to new ideas and ability to take calculated risks.

All people who are gainfully engaged in work manufacturing, distribution or service and other sectors are called entrepreneurs. Again even the founder creator and risk-taker are called entrepreneurs. The term 'entrepreneur' can only be understood with a bearing on economic, psychological, sociological and cultural bearing. The social responsibility is essentially a part of entrepreneurial outlook on life. So the entrepreneur is the key to successful launch of any business. He is the person who perceives the market opportunity and then has the motivation, drive and ability to mobilize resources to meet it.

CHARACTERISTICS OF ENTREPRENEUR: The characteristics of an entrepreneur that contribute to success are the result of his achievement motivation (1) Clear vision, mission and objectives, (2) Self-confidence (3) Technical knowledge (4) Communication ability (5) High energy level (6) Mental ability (7) Human relations ability (8) Business Secrecy (9) Long-term involvement (10) Accept innovation (11) High desire (12) Knowledge of business World (13) Strong financial position (14) Positive thinking (15) Hard work (16) Best organiser (17) Foresightedness (18) Optimistic (19) Motivator (20) Independence (21) Emotional stability (22) Creativity (23) Organisation skill (24) Experience (25) Accept challenges (26) Persistent problem-solver (27) Initiative (28) Risk-taking (29) Accept Ethics and values.

Qualities of an Entrepreneur:

(A) Born Qualities:

(1) Vision inheritance qualities: Family background, Self Inheritance, Physical health, Capacity of self decisions, Wealth of family.

(2) Mental/Psychological Efficiency: Mental health, Initiation, Ready to accept changes, Courageous, Positive attitude, Thinking power, Self confidence, Self respect, Continuous effort.

(3) Other Qualities: Accept challenges, Versatile, Duty and efficiency, Independent, Develop good human relations, Good salesperson, Age, Continuous feedback.

(B) Achieve Qualities:

(4) Knowledge: Business knowledge, Production and administrative knowledge, Technical knowledge, Strategic planning, Knowledge of information technology, Knowledge of Government rules and regulations, Knowledge of competitors,

Motivating employees and customers, Discussion with experts, Data collection and analysis of business environment.

(5) Object Oriented Qualities: Think about conflicting objectives, Healthy competition with self decide objectives, Deep and long involvement in the assignment, Ambitious personality, Ability to bear uncertainty.

(6) Managerial Qualities: Organisational skill, Good administrator, Ideal communication ability, Decide continuous targets, Maintain secrecy of business success.

(7) Financial Matters: Enough provision of finance, Ambition to earn profit, Capacity of moderate risk taking, Research and development, Strong financial position.

(8) Public Relations: Accept social responsibilities, Expert public relation officer Spokesman, Increase company/unit prestige/image, Ability of solving problems continuously.

(9) Other Qualities: Full loyalty, Qualification of specialization, Power of creativity , Employment background, Courage, Good teacher, How to fight with unsuccess , How to make difficult things easy, Educational background, Neutral, Accept personal responsibility about various functions.

The above mention qualities of entrepreneurs, might not be fulfilled by an individual but when we study an entrepreneur, we can come to know about the qualities of an individual.

Functions of an Entrepreneur: An entrepreneur performs many useful functions. He undertakes a venture, assumes risk and earns profit. He is the man having a strong motivation to achieve success. He is self-confident in his entrepreneurial abilities. He exploits opportunities wherever and whenever they arise.

Peter Kilby identified thirteen functions of an entrepreneur, which included some managerial functions also. These functions are as follows: 1. Perceiving market opportunities. 2. Gaining command over scarce resources. 3. Purchasing inputs. 4. Marketing of the products and responding to the competition. 5. Dealing with the public bureaucracy (concessions, licenses and taxes). 6. Managing human relations within the firm. 7. Managing customer and supplier relations. 8. Managing finance. 9. Managing production (control by written records, supervision, coordinating input flows with orders, maintenance).10. Acquiring and overseeing assembly (e.g. of prodn. line of Ford Motors) of the factory. 11. Industrial engineering (minimizing inputs with a given production process) 12. Upgrading process and product quality. 13. Introducing new production techniques and products.

An entrepreneur may have varieties of functions to be performed at the same time but some of the important functions are cited below:

Market survey and research, Analysis of the product, Determination of the business objectives, Human resource development, Undertaking of the business operations, Planning for equipments and material purchase, Completion of promotional formalities, Generations of ideas and scanning of the best and suitable ideas, Raising of necessary funds.

- According to some experts, economists, the functions of an entrepreneur incorporate co-ordination of the business management of the unit (enterprise), risk-taking, controlling the unit, innovation for change, motivation and other related activities. In reality, an entrepreneur has to carry out a combination of these in keeping with time and environment. Truly, he has to consider new ideas, demands and exploit the opportunities, and thereby contribute to technical progress. He is thus a nucleus of high growth of the unit.

TYPES OF ENTREPRENEURS: Clarence Danhof, on the basis of his study of American agriculture, classified entrepreneurs in the manner that, at the initial stage of economic development entrepreneurs have less initiative drive, and as economic development proceeds they become more innovating and enthusiastic. On this basis, he classified entrepreneurs into four categories.

1. Innovating Entrepreneurs, 2. Imitative or Adoptive Entrepreneurs, 3.Fabian Entrepreneurs, 4. Drone Entrepreneurs, 5. Individual and Institutional Entrepreneurs. 6. Entrepreneurship by Inheritance. 7. Technologist Entrepreneurs. 8. Forced Entrepreneurs.

- On the basis of motive, entrepreneurs may be classified in to three categories.

(1) Managing entrepreneurs whose chief goal is security.

(2) Innovating entrepreneurs who want excitement.

(3) Controlling entrepreneurs who above all desire power.

- The entrepreneurs have been broadly classified according to the types of business, use of professional skill, motivation, growth and stages of development. The various types of entrepreneurs are shown as under:

(A) According to the Type of Business: Business entrepreneur, Corporate entrepreneur, Trading entrepreneur, Retail entrepreneur, Service entrepreneur, Industrial entrepreneur micro, small, medium, large, Agricultural entrepreneur-forestry, Dairy, Plantation, Horticulture.

(B) According to the Stages of Development: First generation entrepreneur. Classical entrepreneur, Modern entrepreneur.

(C) According to Gender and Age: Men entrepreneur, Women Entrepreneur, Young Entrepreneur, Middle-aged entrepreneur, Old entrepreneur.

(D) According to the Growth: Growth entrepreneur, Super-growth entrepreneur.

(E) According to the Use of Technology: Technical entrepreneur, Non-technical Entrepreneur, High-tech entrepreneur, Low-tech entrepreneur, Professional entrepreneur.

(F) According to the Sale of Operations: Micro entrepreneur, Small scale entrepreneur, Medium scale entrepreneur, Large scale entrepreneur.

(G) According to the Motivation: Pure entrepreneur, Motivated entrepreneur, Spontaneous entrepreneur, Induced entrepreneur.

(H) Others: Traditional entrepreneur, Modern entrepreneur, Skilled entrepreneur, Non-skilled entrepreneur, Professional entrepreneur, Non-professional entrepreneur, Intrapreneur entrepreneur, Immigrant entrepreneur, Imitating entrepreneur, National entrepreneur, Inherited entrepreneur, Forced entrepreneur, Bureaucratic entrepreneur, International entrepreneur, Multinational entrepreneur.

WHY SHOULD YOU BECOME AN ENTREPRENEUR?

Following are the charms of becoming entrepreneur:

You are your own boss.	You can take your own decisions.
You are independent	You can earn a handsome amount
You can hire the employees.	You acquire an excellence.
You no longer waste your energy and time for looking for good job.	You can use your talent, skills and knowledge for your own and nation's benefit.
Uncertain rewards which can be unlimited.	

MOTIVATING FACTORS FOR STARTING AN INDUSTRIAL UNIT:

Tradition in family, Family background, advice from family members, Advice from business friends, To make use for service experience, Availing facilities of finance, technical and other help by Government institutionsm Desire to meet the demand of market and shortage of supply, Research and survey, Inspired by the success of some of friends/relatives, Self employment, Accept challenges, Profit, Annual turnover

- After training

- Ambition: Personality characteristics, Political support, Socio-cultural factors, Psychological factors and others.

2. ROLE OF AN ENTREPRENEUR

Entrepreneur as a leader, as a risk taker, as a decision taker, as a decision maker and as a business planner

ROLE OF AN ENTREPRENEUR IN ECONOMIC GROWTH AS AN INNOVATOR:

Entrepreneurs mobilize the idle savings of the public through the issues of industrial securities. Investment of public savings in industry results in productive utilization of national resources. Rate of capital formation increases which is essential for rapid economic growth. Thus, an entrepreneur is the creator of economy.

Generation of Employment Opportunities, Complimenting and Supplementing Economic Growth, Bringing about Social Stability, Balanced Regional Development of Industries, Role in Export Promotion, Role in Import Substitution, Forex Earnings: Augmenting and Meeting Local Demand.

Entrepreneurial Motivation: The motivating factors:

P. N. Misra identified nine motivating factors which are as follows:

- Family background
- Educational background
- Occupational experience
- Desire to work independently in manufacturing line
- Desire to branch out to manufacturing
- Availability of raw material and technology
- Assistance from financial institutions
- Assistance from Government
- Other Factors
- Demand of the particular product
- Utilisation of excess money earned from contractual estate business.
- Started manufacturing to facilitate trading /distribution business since the product was in short supply.
- Unstable policy of the foreign government for non-residents.
- No chance for further promotion.

3. ENTREPRENEURSHIP

Introduction:

Entrepreneurship is flourishing in many places around the world. Entrepreneurship started catering in 1980 just as professionalism in management caught up during 1970s. Much has been written in recent times about entrepreneurship and what it represents to business, to the community and to government.

Entrepreneurship, like many other economic concepts, has long been debated. It has been used in various ways and in various senses. The word 'entrepreneurship' has been derived from French, which means 'to undertake'. Today, we call it by various names e.g. 'adventurism', 'risk taking', 'innovating' etc.

Entrepreneurship is the process of identifying opportunities, marshalling the resource needed to take advantage of the opportunities and creating a new venture for the purpose of providing needed products/services to customers and achieving a profit. Entrepreneurship occurs all over the world but it is a particular characteristic of free market economies.

Countries with highest rates of entrepreneurship include the United States, Canada, and Israel and Great Britain etc.

DEFINITIONS OF ENTREPRENEURSHIP:

At a Conference on Entrepreneurship in the U.S.: Entrepreneurship was defined as: "Entrepreneurship is the attempt to create value through recognition of business opportunity, the management of risk taking appropriate to the opportunity, and through the communicative and management skills to mobilize human, financial and material resources necessary to bring a project to fruition."

In the opinion of A. H. Cole: "Entrepreneurship is the purposeful activity of an individual or a group of associated individuals, undertaken to initiate, maintain or aggrandize profit (to increase or improve the power, wealth, influence, or status of somebody or something, especially by a deliberate plan) by production or distribution of economic goods and services.

According to Peter F. Drucker: "Entrepreneurship is neither a science nor an art. It is a practice. It has a knowledge base. Knowledge in entrepreneurship is a means to end. Indeed what constitutes knowledge in practice is largely defined by the ends, that is, by the practice." Entrepreneurship is considerably less risky, if the entrepreneur is methodical and does not violate elementary and well-known rules.

CHARACTERISTICS OF ENTREPRENNERUSHIP:

In above definitions, entrepreneurship refers to the functions performed by an entrepreneur in establishing an enterprise. Just as management is regarded as what managers do, entrepreneurship may be regarded as what entrepreneurs do, entrepreneurship is the act of being an entrepreneur. Entrepreneurship is a process involving various actions to be undertaken to establish an enterprise. It is, thus process of giving birth to a new enterprise.

Clear vision, mission and objective, Decision making, Risk-taking, Innovation, Organisation, Accept challenges, Skillful management, Dynamic view, Analysis of situations, Making the unit a success.

Different Functions: A gap filling function, A function of group level pattern, A function of managerial skill and leadership, A function of status withdrawal, A function of high achievement, Organization building function, A function of social, political and economic structure.

Innovation and Risk Bearing: are regarded as the two basic elements involved in entrepreneurship.

Theories of Entrepreneurship:

The concept of entrepreneurship and its theory have been evolved over a period of more than two centuries. There are different opinions on the emergence of entrepreneurship. These opinions may be classified into three categories: 1.The Economist's View. 2. The Sociologist's View. 3. The Psychologist's View.

ROLE OF ENTREPRENEURSHIP IN ECONOMIC AND INDUSTRIAL DEVELOPMENT:

1. Capital growth/formation. 2. Increase in per capita income. 3. Increase in employment.(Generation of employment). 4. Territorial development (Balanced regional development). 5. Increase in standard of living. (Improvement in living standards) 6. Economic freedom (Economic Independence) 7. Innovation. 8. Research and development. 9. Maximum utilisation of country resources. 10. Decentralisation of industries. 11.

Development of agricultural sector. 12. Development of national human resources. 13. Development of technology. 14. Market share in foreign market. 15. Development of ancillary industry. 16. Market expansion.

THE ANALYTICAL FRAMEWORK OF ENTREPRENEURSHIP:

(1) The Person: Personality, knowledge, education, skill, experience, motives, psychological preferences.

(2) The Environment: Government policy, schemes, availability of resources, infrastructure, competitive pressures, social values, technology, rules and regulations, supplier, business cycle, international-political-economical environment etc.

(3) The Organisation: Structure, policies, rules and regulations, culture, communication system, human resource system, financial and marketing system.

(4) The Task: Vision, Mission, Objectives, perceiving opportunity, providing leadership, marshalling resources.

DIFFERENCE BETWEEN ENTREPRENEUR AND ENTREPRENEURSHIP:

The term "entrepreneur" is often used interchangeably with "entrepreneurship"

ENTREPRENEUR	ENTREPRENEURSHIP
- Refer to a person	- Refer to a process
- Visualiser	- Vision
- Leader	- Leadership
- Planner	- Planning
- Risk-taker	- Risk-taking
- Administrator	- Administration
- Innovator	- Innovation
- Initiator	- Initiative
- Motivator	- Motivation
- Communicator	- Communication
- Programmer	- Action
- Decision-maker	- Decision
- Technician	- Technology
- Organiser	- Organisation
- Creator	- Creation

Entrepreneurship management is basically concerned with the development and co-ordination of entrepreneurial functions. In a way, entrepreneur precedes entrepreneurship.

(Source - Small-scale Industries and Entrepreneurship, By-Vasant Desai, Himalaya Publishing House, Mumbai, 2001, Page No. 403)

ENTREPRENEURSHIP: A ROAD OF DEVELOPMENT IN INDIA

Before independence, entrepreneurship was in abundance amongst Indians but the climate was not conducive. Most of the entrepreneurs emerged from a few business communities like the Banias (Hindu and Jain), Parsees, Gujaratis and the like. By 1911, India had 700 factories mainly in jute, tea and textile industries.

The managing agency houses (Tatas, Birlas, Singhanias, Dalmias, etc.) diversified industrial production after the Second World War. A notable feature of entrepreneurship in the planned period has been the growth of existing entrepreneurs. These entrepreneurs achieved substantial growth with the help of their experience and knowhow. Many firms expanded to harness new and improved technology. Even technicians, rural artisans, engineers, etc. became entrepreneurs. Central and State government and various institutions have provided all types of assistance to small entrepreneurs. Entrepreneurship is now recognized as a source of making money and acquiring social status. Caste and community barriers to mobility have been largely removed. People with diverse background have joined the stream of entrepreneurship. Communities (Brahmins, Nandas, Patels, Kayasthas, Sikhs, Khatris, Aroras) have become new springs of entrepreneurship. Entrepreneurship has dispersed socially as well as geographically. This has been possible due to the development of industrial infrastructure, growth of public sector, foreign collaboration, import substitution and export promotion policies of the government, expansion policies like technical and other education, increasing status of businessman and the like.

Entrepreneur is a person who always seeks for innovation in his business activity, moreover he is ready to take risks in his business activity, e.g. Dhirubhai Ambani (Reliance Industries), Karshanbhai Patel (Nirma). Moreover, we are also having business legends like Birla in our country. The role of an entrepreneur is not smooth as the facts of lots of obstacles. Entrepreneurs should be always ready to accept new challenges in business e.g. opening/ discovering new horizons. The risk taking ability greatly counts in this sense. The entrepreneurs are ready to accept risk (more) there will be more profit (reward).

Thus by analyzing the above points we can say that "entrepreneurship is truly road to development". Entrepreneurship in our country is of great help because it will also help us in reducing ill effects of urbanization and also pollution which is a global concern also. Entrepreneurship will also help to develop villages and rural areas.

An entrepreneur will organize his business in orderly way, in a way he provides a great service, because in India we have scarce resources for which entrepreneurs are in want for effective utilization, a role model for youngsters, e.g. Mukesh Ambani, Kumar Mangalam Birla, Aditya Mittal etc. to name few youngsters of our country can start to walk on their footsteps and achieve prosperity. Entrepreneurship is thus the road to success. It is always better to do a small business then job. Hence self-employment is best employment.But this road to development is not easy. Entrepreneurship will pay you more if you are ready to take more risk. Thus, risk and reward are in direct proportion.

POWERFULL ENTREPRENEURES

Thomas Edison

GE – 1878

Edison is considered one of the most prolific entrepreneurs in history, having founded 14 companies, His biggest entrepreneurial attempt remains GE, one of the largest companies in the world today.

JRD TATA

J.R.D. Tata became the Chairman of Tata sons in 1948. Under him, the companies under the group grew from 15 to 100 and their net worth grew from Rs. 620 million to Rs. 100 billion ! He also started Tata Airlines in 1932 (later renamed Air India)

Akio Morita

Sony 1946
Akio Morita Founded Sony Corp. with just 20 employees, by the name of Tokyo Tsushin kogyo Kabushiki Kaisha. Today, Sony stands for super high- quality!

Narayana Murithy` INFOSYS - 1981

Nagavara Ramarao Narayana Murthy is perhaps the face of information technology for India. He was one of the founders of Infosys Technologies, a global consulting and IT Services company which has taken Indian IT to the world! His is the proud recipient of many global awards for his immaculate entrepreneurial spirit and social vision.

Henry Ford
Revolutionized the transportation, Industries (1860)

Our purpose is to construct and market an automobile for everyday wear and tear Business, professional and family use…a Machine which will be admired by man, woman and child alike for its compactness, its simplicity, its safety, its all-round convenience, and its exceedingly reasonable price."

G.D. Birla

He was responsible for creating India's Second – Largest business group (then) in a very short period of time. Under his grandson Aditya, The group forayed aboard, including in countries like Thailand, Indonesia and Malaysia.

Kasturbhai Lalbhai
He started First large-scale textile mill in 1920 with Rs. 12 lakh when the largest mills were built with not more than Rs. 5 lakh.

Rahul Bajaj

Every group has its uniqueness. I think outs was that we had a huge emphasis on ethics. This came because of my grandfather Jamnalal Bajaj who was extremely close to Mahatma Gandhi say Rahul Bajaj, Chairman, Bajaj Auto

Lala Shri Ram

He was an employee at DCM. During world war II, he set up a company to sell tents to the army. DCM owned 50% of the firm. Lala Shri ram later went to on to acquire complete ownership of DCM

B.M. Munjal

First stab at business was supplying bicycle components in 1944. His biggest came 41 years later when Honda, the world's largest mobike maker, became his joint venture partner. Today, Hero Honda is the world's largest motorcycles producer

Ambani

Licence raj Called for thinking out of the box. That's what Dhirubhai Ambani did. The Intial public offering of Reliance give investor a chance to participate in the success story of what would go on to become India's most valuable company

Adi Godrej

"We always stood for trust, integrity and valued people as our assets. There continue and what has been added is that we have become passionate for success" Says Adi Godrej, Chairman, Godrej Group

Venugopal Dhoot

Videocon's Venugopal Dhoot was quick to grab the advantage of the mid-80s first winds of change. For instance, the colour television industry took off during the 1982 Asian Games and Dhoot clambered onto that bandwagon and gave consumers what they yearned for …

Karsanbhai Patel

Nirma's Karsanbhai Patel was an audacious entrepreneur who took on the marketing machine called Hindustan Lever in the detergents market. Patel battled lever on price, which resulted in the MNC losing market share and Nirma surging ahead of Surf in the 1980s

S.P.OSWAL

Have not looked back since Lachman Das started a socks manufacturing unit in the 1930s

L. N. MITTAL

Although L. N. MITTAL Started working in his   mily's steel-making business,(Mittal Steel).   He was the real entrepreneur behind Mittal Steel's International Success. Today, the company   (having   acquired Arcelor Steel in 2006) is called Arcelor-Mittal, and is the no.1 steel manufacturer in the world controlling 10% of world steel supply.

O.P. Jinda

Warren Buffett

Bill Gates

DR. CRAIG BARRETT

MANOJ KOHLI

RATAN TATA

VIJAY MALYA
CHAIRMAN
KINGFISHER,

ASHWIN DANI
PROMOTER,
ASIAN PAINTS

AZIM   PREMJI
CHAIRMAN,
WIPRO

JAGDISH KHATTAR

MARUTI SUZUKI

R. SESHASAYEE
M.D., ASHOK LEYLAND

PAWAN GOENKA CHAIRMAN,
PRESIDENT,
AUTOMOTIVE SECTOR,
M&M
M&M

INDRA NOOYI,CEO,
COCA-COLA INDIA

ATUL SINGH, C.E.O. & PRESIDENT
PEPSI CO.

REFERENCES:

- Desai Arvindrai N., Environment and Entrepreneurs, Ashish Publishing House, New Delhi, 1989

- Desai Vasant, Dynamics of Entrepreneurial Development and Management, Humalaya Publishing House, Mumbai Reprint (June 2002)

- Desai Vasant, Indian Industry, Himalaya Publishing House, Mumbai First Edition, 1987

- Desai Vasant, Management of a Small Scale Industry, Himalaya Publishing House, Mumbai, Sixth Revised Edition, 1996

- Desai Vasant, Problems and Prospects: for Small Scale Industries, Himalaya Publication

- Desai Vasant, Small Scale Industries and Entrepreneurship, Himalaya Publishing House, Mumbai Third Revised Edition, 1997, Sixth Revised Edition, 2001

- Hathi Yogesh P. and Dr. Rupesh P. Vasani, Entrepreneurship Development, Mahajan Publishing House, Ahmedabad, Second Edition, 2007

- Global Entrepreneurship Monitoring Report: 2002, Entrepreneurship in India, Entrepreneurship Development Institute of India (EDI), China, India, Difference in the details

- Gupta C.B. and Shrinivasan N.P., Entrepreneurship Development in India, Sultanchand & Sons, New Delhi, Reprint 1998

- Gupta R.S.,Sharma B.D., Bhalla N.S., Principles and Practice of Management, Kalyani Publishers, Ludhiana, Reprint, 2000

- Hathi Yogesh P. and Dr. Rupesh P. Vasani, Entrepreneurship Development, Mahajan Publishing House, Ahmedabad, Second Edition, 2007

- Mohan S., Elangovan R., Current Trends in Entrepreneurship, Deep and Deep Publications Pvt.Ltd., New Delhi, 2006

- Sahay A., and Sharma V., Entrepreneurship and New Venture Creation, Excel Books, New Delhi, 2008

- Shrivastav R.P.S., Entrepreneurship Development and Production Management,

Himalaya Publishing House, Mumbai, First Edition, 2007

- Sivayya K.V. and Das V.B.M., Indian Industrial Economy, S. Chand & Company Ltd., New Delhi, Third Edition, 1978

- Subba Rao P., Entrepreneurship and Small Business Management, Discovery Publishing House, New Delhi

PROBLEMS FACED BY WOMEN ENTREPRENEURS

ABSTRACT:

The Hindus worship goddesses as mothers. Indian women are considered as a source of power (shakti) since mythological times. Women have proved themselves very successful entrepreneurs by engaging in one or two income generating ventures within the confines of their homes. The opportunity for developing the home-based small scale entrepreneurship has become more, due to increased level of education among women. The focus of the paper is problem of women entrepreneurs. The paper deals with introduction, problems faced by women entrepreneurs, findings, suggestions and conclusion.

KEY WORDS: Women Entrepreneur, Problems

INTRODUCTION:

Women Entrepreneurship means an act of business ownership and business creation that empowers women economically increases their economic strength as well as position in society.

Women Entrepreneur is a person who accepts challenging role to meet her personal needs and become economically independent. The number of women, who acquire professional skills like engineering, managerial etc., has been increasing manifold today. However, a large proportion of such technically qualified women do not take up employment due to family pressures. There is an urgent need to promote avenues for these women to take up entrepreneurship in the twenty-first century in order to exploit their talents which otherwise go waste.

In reality, women occupy a back seat to men. Moreover, they are revered as mothers, sisters and other social bondages. Many poets have imagined woman's minds as ocean. The upper layers of their minds, like those of the ocean, have turbulent waves. But depths are serene and meditative. Women's minds are essentially steadfast and strong. The truth is acknowledged by the Bhagvad Geeta wherein Lord Krishna describes his manifestation in the feminine quality of Medha or higher intelligence.

OBJECTIVES OF STUDY:

(i) To identify problems faced by women entrepreneurs.

(ii) To examine role of women entrepreneurs

DATA COLLECTION:

In order to achieve the objectives of the present study, the data collected through secondary data. Secondary data was collected from published literature on area of the study. Published literature such as reference books, national and international journals, magazines, newspapers, websites and other published sources were utilized to collect relevant and useful secondary data.

WOMEN ENTREPRENEUR

The status of women in India has been subject to many great changes over the past few millennia. From equal status with men in ancient times through the low points of the medieval period, to the promotion of equal rights by many reformers, the history of women in India has been eventful. In modern India, women have adorned high offices in India including that of the President,

Prime minister, Speaker of the Lok Sabha and Leader of the Opposition. As of 2011, the President of India, the Speaker of the Lok Sabha and the Leader of the Opposition in Lok Sabha (Lower House of the parliament) are all women.

Entrepreneurship has gained currency across the sphere and female- entrepreneurship has become an important section. Women have come forward to establish them as owners and/or manage them. Probably what is noteworthy, is, that women have plunged into the field of entrepreneurship and have been found effective in emerging socio- economic role. A number of them have been engaged in home-based small scale entrepreneurial activities.

Over the last few decades there has been a slow but steady change taking place with respect to development of women. The gross enrolment ratio (GER) for women has increased and women have increasingly come forward to participate in the employment sector. Not only that, women have come forward to establish their own enterprises as well and have become job providers.

MAJOR PROBLEMS OF WOMEN ENTREPRENEURS

Entrepreneurs are playing very important role in the development of economy. They face various problems in day to day work. As the thorns are part of roses, similarly every flourishing business has its own kind of problems. Some of the major problems faced by women entrepreneurs are as under.

RISK BEARER

Women entrepreneurs have less risk bearing capacity due to lack of financial resources and external support.

KNOWLEDGE OF TECHNOLOGY

Information technology is not very common in women areas. Entrepreneurs rely on internal linkages that encourage the flow of goods, services, information and ideas. The intensity of family and personal relationships in women communities can sometimes be helpful but they may also present obstacles to effective business relationships. Business deals may receive less than rigorous objectivity and intercommunity rivalries may reduce the scope for regional cooperation.

FUND ACQUISITION:

Finance is regarded as "life blood" for any enterprise, be it big or small. However, women entrepreneurs suffer from shortage of finance on two counts. Firstly, women do not generally have property on their names to use them as collateral for obtaining funds from external sources. Most of the women entrepreneurs fail to get external funds due to absence of tangible security and credit in the market. The procedure to avail the loan facility is too time-consuming that its delay often disappoints the women entrepreneurs. Lack of finance available to women entrepreneurs is one of the biggest problems which women entrepreneur is born now days especially due to global recession. Major difficulties faced by women entrepreneurs include low level of purchasing power of women consumer so sales volume is insufficient, lack of finance to start business, reduced profits due to competition, pricing of goods and services.

FINDINGS:

- Most of women are still illiterate; illiteracy is the root cause of socio- economic problems.
- Women entrepreneurs face severe completion of large sized organizations and urban entrepreneurs.
- Major sources of finance of women entrepreneurs are loans from regional banks or nationalized banks, but their rate of interest is usually very high.
- The government provides subsidies to women entrepreneurs with high interest rate. Due to the high cost of finance, these subsidies are not giving fruitful results.

SUGGESTIONS:

- The government should provide subsidies to women entrepreneurs with low interest rate. But due to the high cost of finance, these subsidies are not giving fruitful results.
- The NGOs' should provide facilities to women entrepreneurs' like (i) organizing workshops, seminars/conferences on development of women, (ii) organizing training and skill development

activities for women entrepreneurs under Entrepreneurship Development Programme (EDP) of the government, (iii) organizing exhibitions to display the creations/products of women entrepreneurs, (iv) helping / providing women entrepreneurs to avail finance/loans, (v) providing marketing facilities,

➢ Media has continuously focused on issues pertaining to various sections of society including women. It has given lots of strength to women and encouraged them to stand up.

➢ Women entrepreneur should understand continuous innovation and progress in technology like Mobile telephone and Internet

➢ Women entrepreneur should risk bearer. Risk bearing is an essential requisite of a successful entrepreneur.

CONCLUSION:

Due to 21st Century and changing environment, women have now realized their own strength not only in terms of providing gainful assistance to men in running the family but also perform the roles played earlier by men in various fields, one of which include entrepreneurship. They want their works to be accounted properly and the worth known to the world. Entrepreneurs are playing very important role in the development of economy. Women entrepreneur should take risk for running successful business.

REFERENCES

➢ Desai Vasant, Dynamics of Entrepreneurial Development and Management, Humalaya Publishing House, Mumbai Reprint (June 2002)

➢ Desai Vasant, Indian Industry, Himalaya Publishing House, Mumbai First Edition, 1987

➢ Kothari C.R., Research Methodology Methods and Techniques, New Delhi, Wishwa Prakashan, Second Edition.

- Patel Brijesh, Chavda Kirit International Journal of Advance Research in Computer Science and Management Studies Volume 1, Issue 2, July 2013 pg. 28-37

- Singh Ranbir, International Journal of Democratic And Development Studies (IJDDS), VOL. 1(1): 45-58

- Nandanwar Kalpana P. (2011), Role of Women Entrepreneurship in Women Development, International Referred Research Journal, ISSN-0974-2832, Vol. II, ISSUE-26, March.

- Santhi N. and Rajesh Kumar S. (2011), Entrepreneurship Challenges and Opportunities in India, International Journal of Industrial Engineering and Management Science, Vol. 1, Special Issue, December.

- www.iosrjournals.org

- http://www.scribd.com/doc/26661470/Women-Entrepreneurship-in-India

- http:/www.rcmss.org/ijdds/Vol.1/No.1/pdf

A STUDY ON HUMAN RESOURCE PROBLEMS OF ENTREPRENEURS

ABSTRACT :

"Think Business, Think Gujarat." Gujarat has witnessed impressive industrial development since its formation as a state in 1960. The industries in Gujarat produce different of products. An entrepreneur is a person who undertakes industrial venture. He is a change agent. Success of any Entrepreneurs is based on his or her human resource. The present study is focused on Entrepreneurs and human resource. There are different objectives, hypothesis, sources of data etc of this study. The present study was carried out 150 Entrepreneurs of selected chemical and engineering industrial units in preferred cities of Gujarat like- Ahmedabad, Vadodara, Surat and Rajkot. Majority of Entrepreneurs face human resource problems such as balance between supply and demand (short), absenteeism / high turnover, stress and conselling, technical knowledge, negative attitude of labour force, leave, wages and salary. Problems related to H.R.D. are quite visible in Ahmedabad, the problems at Rajkot is more visible as compared to other cities. So accept latest modern transparent scientific techiniques of selection of H.R. Know human psychology, make right decisions and give gift of motivation to your H.R. Select knowledgable, intelligent, creative industries minister for central and state Government. Give theoretical + Practical knowledge to students.

So Entrepreneurs don't lose 'Human Touch', Opportunities well become across your way every day.

Key Words : Entrepreneurs, Human Resource, Hypothesis, Field work,SSI - MSI - LSI, Absenteeism, Technical Knowledge, Scientific, Counselling

INTRODUCTION

"Think Business, Think Gujarat."

Gujarat has witnessed impressive industrial development since its formation as a state in 1960. Gujarat has achieved the distinction of being the highly industrial developed state in India. The industries in Gujarat produce different of products. During the period 1960 - 2012, Gujarat established itself as a leader in various industrial sector like Textile, Engineering, Chemical, Pharmaceuticals, Dairy, Dyes, Cement, Gems & Jewellery etc.

The Entrepreneurs is one of the most important inputs in the economic development of a country or of regions within the country. Entrepreneurs have creative and innovative ideas and ability to recognize it, initiate and exploit an economic opportunity. Entrepreneurs is a person who undertakes industrial venture. Industriliast is a change agent. He searches and accepts innovation. Minimum input, maximum output and quality maintenance that person Entrepreneurs.

Success of any Entrepreneurs is based on his or her human resource. Our great Entrepreneurs. Late Shri

J.R.D. Tata has remarked, "well-experienced, imaginative and sincere employees are the most valuable assets of a business."

The term human resource (H.R.) means, "the total knowledge, skills, creative ability, talents and aptitudes of an organisation's workforce as well as the value, attitudes and beliefs of the individuals involved." The present study focused on Entrepreneurs and human resources problems. Details as follows.

(A) RESERACH METHODOLOGY:

The research methodology is used for collection, analysis and tabulation of data for the research. The selected tools are being utilized for the particular research, following is the detailed design used in the research.

(B) PROBLEMS OF THE STUDY:

"A study on Human Resource Problems of Entrepreneurs"

(C) RATIONALE OF THE STUDY:

The present study focuses on 'Entrepreneurs and Human Resource Problems' The research study attempts to explore various area associated with 'Entrepreneurs and Human Resource (H.R.)' in selected chemical and engineering industrial units in the Gujarat.

(D) Objectives of the research study :

(1) To study and describe the human resource (HR) problems of 'Entrepreneurs/entrepreneus' of selected chemical and engineering industrial units in preferred cities of Gujarat like - Ahmedabad, Vadodara, Surat and Rajkot.

(2) To analyze and ascertain various problems faced by the sample units of the study.

(3) To study the prospect of entrepreneurs of selected industrial units.

(4) To collect valuable suggestions.

(E) Hypothesis :

(1) H_0 = Entrepreneurs of Selected Chemical and engineering industrial units in preferred cities of Gujarat are not suffering from several problems related to 'Human Resource' (HR)

H_1 = Entrepreneurs of selected Chemical and engineering industrial units in preferred cities of

Gujarat are suffering from several problems related to 'Human Resouce' (HR.)

(2) H_0 = Several industrial units haven't similar problems.

H_1 = Several industrial units have similar problems.

(F) Research Design :

The study is based on descriptive type of research.

(G) Sources of Data :

In order to achieve the objective of present study, there are two types of data collection methods.

(A) Primary Data   (B) Secondary Data

(A) Primary Data: Primary data was collected from the Entrepreneurs of selected chemical and engineering industrial units in prepferred cities of Gujarat through interview, personal investigation, visits etc. A structured questionnaire was used to collect the primary data (i) Entrepreneurs (ii) Human Resource(HR)

(B) Secondary Data : Secondary data was collected from various publications.

(H) Data collection methods:

In this study, I used a personal survey method which is the face to face questioning and answering to Entrepreneurs.

(I) FIELD WORK: The present study was carried out at selected chemical and engineering industrial units in prefered cities of Gujarat like-Ahmedabad Vadodara, Surat and Rajkot.

(J) SAMPLING PLAN:

(A) Sampling methods: Non probability convenience sampling methods was used.

(B) Sample size: Sample of one hundred fifty (150) industrial units entrepreneurs include 75 unit of chemical and 75 units of engineering has been selected for the study.

(C) Sample unit: Entrepreneurs of selected chemical and engineering industrial units in preferred cities of Gujarat state.

(K) Significance of the study:

India started its quest for industrial development after independence in 1947. The industrial policy resolution on 1948 maked the beginning of evolution of the indian industrial policy. The industrial policy resolution of 1956 gives the public sector strategic role in the economy. With the introduction of the new industrial policy in 1991, a sustantial programme of degregulation has been undertaken.

Significance also lies in understanding the approach of Entrepreneurs.

- To understand human resource (HR) problems of chemical and engineering industrial units in preferred, cities of Gujarat like - Ahmedabad, Vadodara, Surat and Rajkot.

- Identifying future prospects.

- Getting help in future planning of development.

- Understanding various problems: from the point of views of current & new Entrepreneurs, industrial executives, local authority, employment and other industries cities.

- The study is important in understanding entrepreneurs motivation and leadership.

- Government eye view policy and administrative decisions.

(L) Limitations of the study:

As every coin has two side, the research study also has two side. There are certain limitations which deceive the object of the study.

(1) The study is based on Entrepreneurs of selected chemical and engineering industrial units in Gujarat.

(2) The study is based on preferred cities of Gujarat like- Ahmedabad, Vadodara, Surat and Rajkot.

(3) The study is based on human resource problems only.

(4) The sample size prefixed for the research study was one hundred fifty (150) industrial units in Gujarat which are limited concerns.

(5) Time, finance and co-operation factors are also responsible for problems and delay.

This chapter provides detailed information about the profile of the entrepreneurs of selected Chemical and Engineering units in Gujarat. It gives a base of selected entrepreneurs of cities like Ahmedabad, Vadodara, Surat and Rajkot.

Profile of entrepreneurs:

In this section the profile of the respondent has been discussed in detail.

The below table No. 1 shows that majority of the respondents are in the age group of 46-55 years. There are more respondents (64%) of the Engineering Industry in the 36-45 years age group. While there are 55% respondents of the Chemical Industry in the age group of 46-55 years.

Table: Age-wise Distribution

Details	Chemical	Engineering	Total
Age-wise Distribution	T = 75	T = 75	N = 150
26-35 years	5(41.7)	7(58.3)	12 (8.0)
36-45 years	18(36.0)	32(64.0)	50(33.3)
46-55 years	33(55.0)	27(45.0)	60(40.0)
Above 56 years	18(67.7)	9(33.3)	27(18.0)
No reply	1(100.00)	-	1(0.7)

(Figures in parenthesis are in percentage)

The Gender distribution shows that almost all the respondents are male. Out of 150 the numbers of male respondents are 147, while 3 are women

Profile of Selected Industries:

In this section detailed profile of the selected Industries has been discussed.

In Table No. 5 it can be seen that the size of the Industry shows that Small Scale Industries are the maximum, which is 84.7% while the least are LSI with 7.3%. The majority of both the Chemical and Engineering Industries fall under the SSI category. Whereas only 8% of the totals are MSI, of which only 2 are Chemical Industries.

Table: Details of the Industry

Details	Chemical	Engineering	Total
Size of Industry	T = 75	T = 75	N = 150
Small Scale Industry (SSI)	68(53.50)	59(46.50)	127(84.7)
Medium Scale Industry (MSI)	2(16.70)	10(83.30)	12(8.0)
Large Scale Industry (LSI)	5(45.50)	6(54.50)	11(7.3)

(Figures in parenthesis are in percentage)

Majority of the selection of Industry has been done from Ahmedabad, followed by Rajkot, Baroda and Surat.

Graph: City-wise Selection of Industries

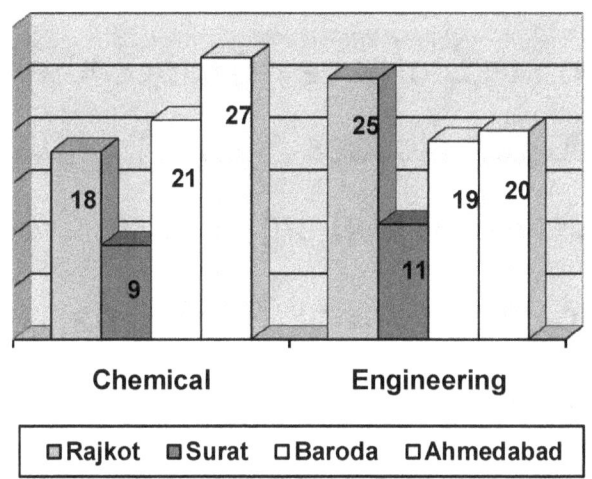

Table: Number of Employees

Details	Chemical	Engineering	Total
Total Employees in the Industry	T = 75	T = 75	N = 150
1 to 50	65(51.20)	62(48.80)	127(84.66)
51 to 100	8(72.70)	3(27.30)	11(7.33)
101 to 200		3(100.00)	3(2.0)
201 to 400	2(50.0)	2(50.0)	4(2.67)
401 to 500		1(100.00)	1(0.67)
Above 500		3(100.00)	3(2.0)
No reply		1(100.00)	1(0.67)

(Figures in parenthesis are in percentage)

Nearly 85% of the respondents have reported to have employees between 1 to 50. This number has been almost equally reported by the Chemical and Engineering Industries. This is followed by 51 to 100 employees by 7.3% of the respondents. Some of the Industries have reported to have 101 to 200 employees (2%), 201 to 400 employees (2.7%), 401 to 500 employees (0.67%), above 500 employees (2%).

Table: Ranking of Personnel Problems - Balance between Employee supply and demand (Short)

Details	Chemical	Engineering	Total
	T = 73	T = 73	N = 146
Strongly Agree	3(12.5)	21(87.5)	24(16.4)
Agree	5(41.7)	7(58.3)	12(8.2)
Undecided	56(65.1)	30(34.9)	86(58.9)
Disagree	6(60.0)	4(40.0)	10(6.9)
Strongly Disagree	3(21.4)	11(78.6)	14(9.6)

(Figures in parenthesis are in percentage)

16.40% of the respondents *strongly agree* that balance between employee supply and demand is a personnel problem, out of which 87.50% are of Engineering

Industry. 8.2% respondents *agree* with this problem with a majority from Engineering Industry. 58.90 respondents are *undecided* about this problem of which the majority are from Chemical Industry (65.10%). 6.9% respondents *disagree* with a ratio of 60-40 from both industries and 9.6% respondents *strongly disagree* of which 78.60% are from the Engineering Industry.

Table: Ranking of Personnel Problems - Absenteeism/High turnover

Details	Chemical	Engineering	Total
	T = 73	T = 73	N = 146
Strongly Agree	6(46.2)	7(53.8)	13(8.9)
Agree	28(46.7)	32(53.3)	60(41.1)
Undecided	11(44.0)	14(56.0)	25(17.1)
Disagree	28(58.3)	20(41.7)	48(32.9)

(Figures in parenthesis are in percentage)

41.10% respondents *agree* that absenteeism/high turnover is a personnel problem of which majority are from the Engineering Industry with 53.30%. 8.90% respondents *strongly agree* to this of which 53.8% are from the Engineering Industry. 17.10% respondents remain *undecided*, while 32.90% respondents *disagree* to this with majority being from Chemical Industry at 58.30%.

Table: Ranking of Personnel Problems - Stress and Counseling

Details	Chemical	Engineering	Total
	T = 73	T = 73	N = 146
Strongly Agree	6(35.3)	11(64.7)	17(11.6)
Agree	28(51.9)	26(48.1)	54(37.0)
Undecided	19(48.7)	20(51.3)	39(26.7)
Disagree	20(58.8)	14(41.2)	34(23.3)
Strongly Disagree		2(100.0)	2(1.4)

(Figures in parenthesis are in percentage)

54 (37%) respondents agree that stress and counseling is personnel problem. 17 respondents strongly agree to this. In the above cases, Chemical Industry is the dominant in first one with 51.90% and Engineering industry is dominant in the second with 64.70%. 39 respondents remain undecided. 34 respondents disagree with this in which the ratio of the both the Industries is about 60-40 between Chemical and

Engineering. 2 Engineering Industry respondents strongly disagree with this.

Table: Ranking of Personnel Problems - Technical knowledge

Details	Chemical	Engineering	Total
	T = 73	T = 73	N = 146
Strongly Agree	12(33.3)	24(66.7)	36(24.7)
Agree	38(62.3)	23(37.7)	61(41.8)
Undecided	19(50.0)	19(50.0)	38(26.0)
Disagree	3(33.3)	6(66.7)	9(6.1)
Strongly Disagree	1(50.0)	1(50.0)	2(1.4)

(Figures in parenthesis are in percentage)

Technical knowledge is one of the factors of personnel problems, which is *agreed* by 41.80% respondents. The majority is from the Chemical Industry with 62.30%. 24.70% respondents *strongly agree* with this but the majority is Engineering Industry at 66.70%. 6.10% respondents *disagree* with the dominance of Engineering Industry at 66.70%. 1 respondent from each

Industry strongly *disagreed*. 26% respondents remain *undecided*.

HYPOTHESIS TESTING

Paired Samples t-Tests

When two samples are involved and the values for each sample are collected from the same individuals (i.e. each individual gives us two values, one for each of the two groups), or the samples come from matched pairs of individuals then a paired-samples t-test may be an appropriate statistic to use.

The paired samples t-test can be used to determine if two means are different from each other when the two samples that the means are based on were taken from the matched individuals or the same individuals.

The t-test has been done using SPSS. The command for the paired samples t tests is found at Analyze | Compare Means | Paired-Samples T Test (this is shorthand for clicking on the Analyze menu item at the top of the window, and then clicking on Compare Means from the drop down menu, and Paired-Samples T Test. The hypothesis tested was:

Hypothesis - I

H_o – Entrepreneurs of selected chemical and engineering industrial units are not suffering from several problems related to personnel and marketing.

H_1 – Entrepreneurs of selected chemical and engineering industrial units are suffering from several problems related to personnel and marketing.

Personnel Problems by Type of Industry

Table: Does there exist any personnel problems in the industries:

Paired sample statistics	Mean	N	Std. Deviation	Std. Error Mean
Type	1.5	150	0.502	0.041
Do you have any Personnel Problems	1.03	150	0.162	0.013

Paired Samples Correlations	N	Correlation	Sig.	
TYPE - Do you have any Personnel Problems	150	0	1	

Paired Samples Test	Mean	Std. Deviation	Std. Error Mean	95% Confidence Interval of the Difference		t	df	Sig. (2-tailed)
				Lower	Upper			
TYPE - Do you have any Personnel Problems	0.47	0.527	0.043	0.39	0.56	10.999	149	0

A paired samples *t* test managed to reveal a statistically reliable difference between the mean of type of industries (M = 1.5, s = 0.502) and personnel problems (M = 1.03, s = 0.162) that the industry faces, *t*(149) = 10.999, *p* = .0, α = 1.

FINDINGS:

While discussing with 150 Entrepreneurs of selected chemical and engineering units in Gujarat. Entrepreneurs were interviewed and requirested to answer the questionnaire. They were conduct personnally to avoid misunderstanding. On the basis of data analysis and interpretation many findings where found, the finding are as follows.

- Majority of the respondents are in the age group of 46-55 years.

- There are more respondents (64%) of the engineering industry in the 36-45 years age group.

- While there are 55% respondents of the chemical indeustry in the age group of 46-55 years.

- Almost all respondents are male.

- The majority of both the chemical and engineering industries fall under the SSI category.

- Majority of the selection of industry has been done from Ahmedabad, followed by Vadodara, Surat and Rajkot.

- Nearly 85% of respondents have reported to have employees between 1 to 50. This number has been almost equally reported by the chemical and engineering industries. Some of the industries have reported to have 101 to 200 employees.

- Majorits of chemical and Engineering industries Entrepreneurs face human resource problems such as balance between employee supply and demand (short), absenteeism/high turnover, stress and counseling, technical knowledge negative attitude of labour force, leave, wages and salary.

- Problems related to human resource department are quite visible in Ahmedabad for chemical industry and in engineering industry, the problems at Rajkot is more visible as compared to other cities.

SUGGESTIONS

- Provide training and motivation to female for entrepreneurship development and give zender special assistance to them.

- Extend special facilities to small scale industry (SSI) for growth and development. e.g. Government program, tax benefits, selection of location, finance etc.

- Men you are free think about your industry, business and develop plan in your mind, dream for highest success.

- Entrepreneurs please develop personal relations and give personal touch to each and every trnasaction with your human resource. Study each and every one.

- Give equal weightage to highest satisfaction of human resource and yourself.

- Collect lots of knowledge about human psychology, then think and make right decision, each and every moment teach you. Welcome innovation in H.R. Dept. Give gift of motivation to your human resource.

- Draw your vision, mission and objectives of industry and future strategy.

- Discuss problems with experts, technologists, advocate, chartered accountant and collect guidance from them and make your own decisions.

- Accept latest modern transparent techniques of employee supply and demand balance, absenteeism/high turnover, stress and counseling technical knowledge, time schedule. Please obtain and maintain satisfactory and satisfied workforce in an organisation.

- Think positively on problems. 'Problems are not problems but your work' Motivate your human resource through carrer planning, provide career guidance, recognisation, rewards, discuss about specific matter, study human psychology etc.

- Redress Entrepreneurs, managers, supervisors, and workers stress through expert courseling. Live in present situation, develop and provide entertainment facilities, motivation, celebrate festival, one picnic per year, provide crucial health excercises equipments, arrange yoga classes etc.

- Maintain balance between human resource expectations and job expectation description. Create your organisational culture, collect data about different changes.
- Problems of skilled human resource of engineering industry high at Rajkot, Ahmedabad, Vadodara and Surat. Open new or provide technical training schools, colleges and ITI, professional study centers at different cities.
- Give qualitative, practical and theoretical knowledge to students then create, excellent work force for both the industries.
- Establish special research and information centre at Rajkot for engineering industyr. In Rajkor, extend special facilities to chemical industry, then they develop, otherwise Rajkot is only engineering cluster.
- Provide special travelling mobility at Rajkot start national/ international level special air services.
- Select knowledgeable, creative, intelligent, industries minister for central and state Government.

- Let's come together for global opportunities, beneficial partnership and sustainable growth.

CONCLUSION:

With reference to one hundred fifty Entrepreneurs of selected chemical and engineering industrial units in Gujarat. Minimum input, maximum output and quality maintain that person entrepreneur/Entrepreneurs.

Balance between employee supply and demand absenteeism/high turnover, stress and counseling, technical knowledge, aquaring right staff, are major Human Resource problems of both the industry.

As Entrepreneurs determine the problem evaluate the data and facts at hand, identify the solutions and select the best ones for implementation. Don't lose 'Human Touch', opportunities will become across your way' everyday.

Eighty percent of your results would be achieved by sorting out twenty percent of your problems learn to priorities effectively.

REFERENCES:

➤ Desai Vasant, Dynamics of Entrepreneurial Development and Management, Humalaya Publishing House, Mumbai Reprint (June 2002)

➤ Desai Vasant, Indian Industry, Himalaya Publishing House, Mumbai First Edition, 1987

➤ Kothari C.R., Research Methodology Methods and Techniques, New Delhi, Wishwa Prakashan, Second Edition.

www.ingramcontent.com/pod-product-compliance
Lightning Source LLC
Chambersburg PA
CBHW080832180526
45168CB00006B/2659